Deportes y actividades/Sports and Activities

# ¡Vamos a jugar al fútbol americano!
# Let's Play Football!

## por/by Jan Mader

**Editora consultora/Consulting Editor:** Gail Saunders-Smith, PhD

**Consultora/Consultant:** Kymm Ballard, MA
Consultora de Educación Física, Atletismo y Medicina Deportiva
Departamento de Instrucción Pública de Carolina del Norte/
Physical Education, Athletics, and Sports Medicine Consultant
North Carolina Department of Public Instruction

CAPSTONE PRESS
a capstone imprint

Pebble Plus is published by Capstone Press,
1710 Roe Crest Drive, North Mankato, Minnesota 56003.
www.capstonepub.com

 Books published by Capstone Press are manufactured with paper
containing at least 10 percent post-consumer waste.

*Library of Congress Cataloging-in-Publication Data*
Mader, Jan (Janet G)
 ¡Vamos a jugar al fútbol americano! = Let's play football!  / by Jan Mader.
    p. cm. —(Pebble plus Deportes y actividades/Sports and activities)
 Includes index.
 Summary: "Simple text and photographs present the skills, equipment, and safety concerns of football—in
both English and Spanish"—Provided by publisher.
 ISBN 978-1-4296-8244-2 (library binding)
 1. Football—Juvenile literature. I. Title. II. Title: Let's play football!
 GV950.7.M253 2012
 796.332—dc23                                                    2011028800

**Editorial Credits**
Amber Bannerman, editor; Strictly Spanish, translation services; Juliette Peters, set designer; Bobbi J. Wyss,
    book designer; Eric Manske, bilingual book designer; Kelly Garvin, photo researcher/photo editor;
    Kathy McColley, production specialist

**Photo Credits**
Capstone Press/Karon Dubke, 10–11 (football); TJ Thoraldson Digital Photography, cover, 1 (kids with football),
    5, 8–9, 13, 19 (player)
Corbis/Kelly-Mooney Photography, 14–15; Michael Kim, 16–17; Michael Prince, 18–19 (background);
    Tom Stewart, 21
Getty Images Inc./John Giustina, 6–7
Photodisc, 1 (clouds)
Shutterstock/Greg Soybelman, 10–11 (goalposts)

## Note to Parents and Teachers

The Deportes y actividades/Sports and Activities set supports national physical
education standards related to recognizing movement forms and exhibiting a physically
active lifestyle. This book describes and illustrates football in both English and Spanish.
The images support early readers in understanding the text. The repetition of words and
phrases helps early readers learn new words. This book also introduces early readers
to subject-specific vocabulary words, which are defined in the Glossary section. Early
readers may need assistance to read some words and to use the Table of Contents,
Glossary, Internet Sites, and Index sections of the book.

Printed in the United States of America in North Mankato, Minnesota.
102011    006405CGS12

# Table of Contents

# Tabla de contenidos

# Playing Football

Punt, pass, run, tackle!
Toss the football
with your friends.

# Juguemos al fútbol americano

¡Patea, lanza, corre, taclea!
Juega a la pelota
con tus amigos.

One team runs and passes
down the field. The other
team tries to stop them.

---

Un equipo corre y pasa hacia
delante en la cancha de juego.
El otro equipo trata de detenerlo.

Players get the ball
to the end zone.
Touchdown!
They score six points.

---

Los jugadores llevan la pelota
a la zona de anotación.
¡Anotación!
Ellos anotan seis puntos.

Players kick the ball through
the goalposts. They score
three points. Field goal!

———————————————————

Los jugadores patean la pelota
a través de postes de anotación.
Ellos anotan tres puntos.
¡Gol de campo!

# Equipment

Footballs are made of strong
brown leather. White laces
help players hold on to
the ball.

# Equipo

Las pelotas de fútbol americano
están hechas de cuero marrón fuerte.
Cordones blancos ayudan a los
jugadores a sostener la pelota.

Football fields have many
white lines. Goalposts stand
at each end of the field.

---

Las canchas de fútbol americano
tienen muchas líneas blancas.
Los postes de anotación están
ubicados en cada extremo
de la cancha.

# Safety

Helmets protect players'
heads from tackles and hits.
Mouth guards protect
their teeth.

# Seguridad

Los cascos protegen la cabeza
de los jugadores de tacleos y
golpes. Los protectores para
la boca protegen sus dientes.

16

Thick pads keep players'
bodies safe. Shoes with
cleats help keep players
from slipping.

---

Las hombreras gruesas mantienen
protegido el cuerpo de los jugadores.
Los zapatos con tapones ayudan
a que los jugadores no se resbalen.

# Having Fun

Come kick, run,

score, and cheer.

Let's play football!

# Vamos a divertirnos

Ven y patea, corre,

anota y alienta.

¡Vamos a jugar

al fútbol americano!

# Glossary

**cleats**—small tips on the bottom of shoes that help players stop or turn quickly

**end zone**—the area at the end of the field; when a team gets the ball into the end zone, they score a touchdown

**field goal**—a three-point score in a football game

**goalpost**—a post that marks each end of the field; players get points for getting the ball through the goalposts

**protect**—to keep safe

**punt**—a kick where the ball is dropped from the hands and kicked before it touches the ground

**tackle**—to stop another player by knocking them to the ground

**touchdown**—a six-point score in a football game

# Internet Sites

FactHound offers a safe, fun way to find Internet sites related to this book. All of the sites on FactHound have been researched by our staff.

Here's all you do:

Visit *www.facthound.com*

Type in this code: 9781429682442

Check out projects, games and lots more at
**www.capstonekids.com**

# Glosario

**la anotación**—puntaje de seis puntos en un partido de fútbol americano

**el gol de campo**—una anotación de tres puntos en un partido de fútbol americano

**la patada de despeje**—una patada donde la pelota se deja caer de las manos y se la patea antes de que caiga al suelo

**los postes de anotación**—un poste que marca cada extremo de la cancha; los jugadores obtienen puntos al patear la pelota entre los postes de anotación

**proteger**—mantener seguro

**taclear**—detener a otro jugador tirándolo al suelo

**los tapones**—pequeñas puntas en la suela de los zapatos que ayudan a los jugadores a detenerse o girar rápidamente

**la zona de anotación**—el área al final de la cancha; cuando un equipo lleva la pelota a la zona de anotación, marcan una anotación

# Sitios de Internet

FactHound brinda una forma segura y divertida de encontrar sitios de Internet relacionados con este libro. Todos los sitios en FactHound han sido investigados por nuestro personal.

Esto es todo lo que tienes que hacer:

Visita *www.facthound.com*

Ingresa este código: 9781429682442

# Index

# Índice